Talking Hands
ACTIONS

ACCIONES

The Child's World

Published in the United States of America by The Child's World®
PO Box 326, Chanhassen, MN 55317-0326
800-599-READ
www.childsworld.com

Cover / frontispiece: left, right—RubberBall Productions.

Interior: 3, 4, 5, 10, 11, 12, 15, 16, 23—RubberBall Productions; 6, 7, 9, 19—Stockdisc; 8—Tom & Dee Ann McCarthy / Corbis; 13, 18—Brand X Pictures; 14—Norbert Schaefer / Corbis; 17—K. Solveig / zefa / Corbis; 20—Photodisc; 21, 22—Image Source.

The Child's World®: Mary Berendes, Publishing Director

Editorial Directions, Inc.: E. Russell Primm, Editorial Director; Katie Marsico, Project Editor and Managing Editor; Caroline Wood, Editorial Assistant; Javier Millán, Proofreader; Cian Laughlin O'Day, Photo Researcher and Selector

The Design Lab: Kathleen Petelinsek, Art Director; Julia Goozen, Art Production

LIBRARY OF CONGRESS CATALOGING-IN-PUBLICATION DATA
Petelinsek, Kathleen.
    Actions = Acciones / by Kathleen Petelinsek and E. Russell Primm; content advisers, June Prusak and Carmine L. Vozzolo.
      p. cm. — (Talking hands)
    Summary: Provides illustrations of American Sign Language signs and Spanish and English text for various action words.
    In English, Spanish, and American Sign Language.
    ISBN-10: 1-59296-679-9 (lib. bdg. : alk. paper)
    1. American Sign Language—Verb—Juvenile literature. 2. Spanish language—Verb—Juvenile literature. 3. English language—Verb—Juvenile literature. I. Primm, E. Russell, 1958- . II. Title. III. Title: Acciones. IV. Series: Petelinsek, Kathleen. Talking hands.
HV2476.P45 2006
419'.782421—dc22   2006009034

NOTE TO PARENTS AND EDUCATORS:

The understanding of any language begins with the acquisition of vocabulary, whether the language is spoken or manual. The books in the Talking Hands series provide readers, both young and old, with a first introduction to basic American Sign Language signs. Combining close photo cues and simple, but detailed, line illustration, children and adults alike can begin the process of learning American Sign Language. In addition to the English word and sign for that word, we have included the Spanish word. The addition of the Spanish word is a wonderful way to allow children to see multiple ways (English, Spanish, signed) to say the same word. This is also beneficial for Spanish-speaking families to learn the sign even though they may not know the English word for that object.

Let these books be an introduction to the world of American Sign Language. Most languages have regional dialects and multiple ways of expressing the same thought. This is also true for sign language. We have attempted to use the most common version of the signs for the words in this series. As with any language, the best way to learn is to be taught in person by a frequent user. It is our hope that this series will pique your interest in sign language.

Walk
Caminar

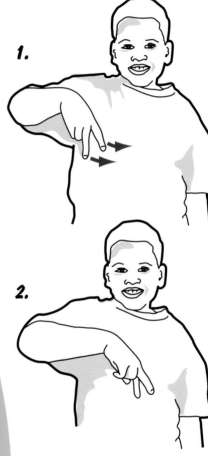

1.

2.

Move index and middle fingers to show how someone's legs move when they are walking.

Mover los dedos índice y medio para indicar como se mueven las piernas cuando se camina.

3

Run
Correr

1.

Interlock left index finger with right thumb. Slightly curl right index finger and left thumb at the same time. Repeat.

Entrelace el dedo índice izquierdo con el pulgar derecho. Enrosque ligeramente el dedo índice derecho y el pulgar izuierdo a la misma vez. Repetir.

Jump
Saltar

1.

2.

Index and middle fingers curl up as entire right hand moves up.

Los dedos índice y medio se enroscan hacia arriba a la vez que la mano derecha se mueve hacia arriba.

Stand
Parado/Estar de Pie

1.

Tips of index and middle fingers of right hand touch palm of left hand.

Las yemas de los dedos índice y medio de la mano derecha tocan la palma de la mano izquierda.

Sit
Sentado

1.

2.

Index and middle fingers of right hand move down to index and middle fingers of left hand.

Los dedos índice y medio de la mano derecha se mueven hacia abajo a los dedos índice y medio de la mano izquierda.

Fall
Caer

1.

2.

Index and middle fingers of right hand fall off of left palm.

Los dedos índice y medio de la mano derecha se desprenden de la palma de la mano izquierda.

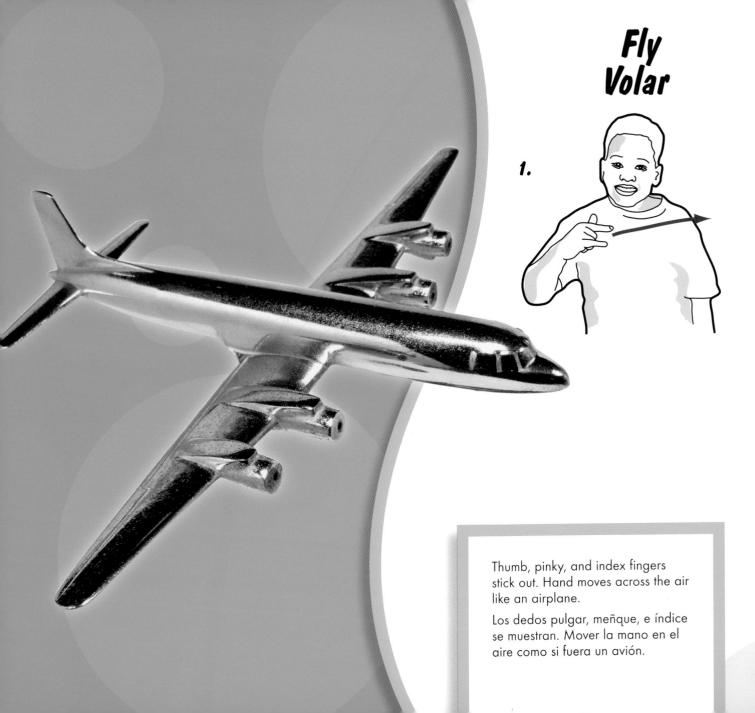

Fly
Volar

1.

Thumb, pinky, and index fingers
stick out. Hand moves across the air
like an airplane.

Los dedos pulgar, meñque, e índice
se muestran. Mover la mano en el
aire como si fuera un avión.

Kick
Patear

1.

2.

Flat right hand (with palm facing the floor) moves up to flat left hand.

Mover la mano derecha plana (palma mirando hacia el piso) hacia arriba de la palma de la mano izquierda.

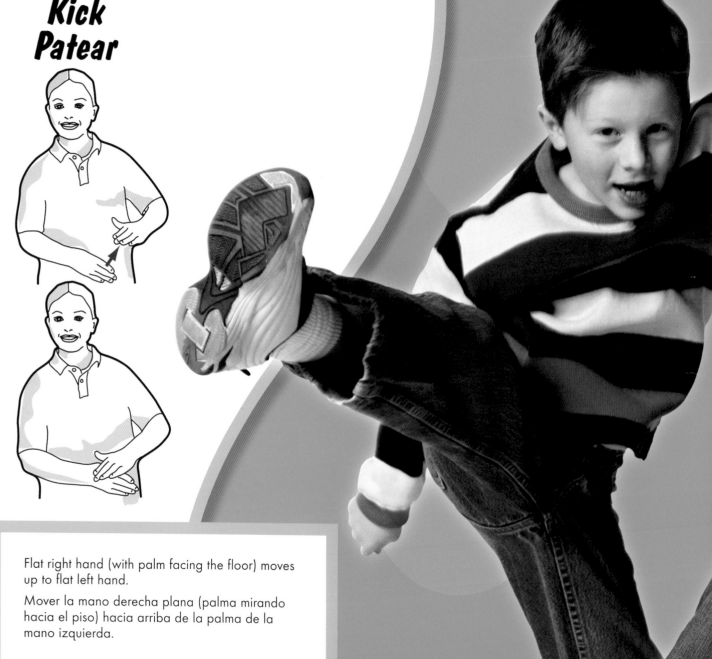

Dance
Bailar

1.

Right hand makes an upside-down "V" hand shape and swings back and forth over left hand.

Formar la "V" boca abajo con la mano derecha y mover hacia adelante y hacia atrás sobre la mano izquierda.

Bounce
Rebotar/Saltar

1.

Flat right hand (with palm facing toward the floor) moves up and down as if bouncing a ball.

Mover la mano derecha plana (palma mirando hacia el piso) para arriba y para abajo como si estuviera rebotando una pelota.

12

Swing
Oscilar

1.

2.

Index and middle fingers of right hand rest on index and middle fingers of left hand. Together, both hands swing away and toward body.

Los dedos índice y medio de la mano derecha descansan en los dedos índice y medio de la mano izquierda. Simultaneamente oscilar ambas manos hacia adentro y hacia afuera del cuerpo.

Stir
Mover/Revolver

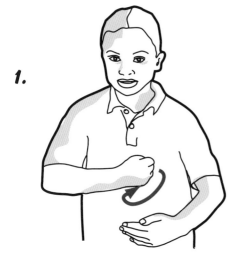

1.

Right hand moves in a circle, as if stirring. Left arm scoops downward, as if holding a bowl.

Mover la mano derecha en forma circular como si estuviera revolviendo. El brazo izquierdo se dealiza hacia abajo, como si estuviera susteniendo un tazón.

Roll
Revolcarse

1.

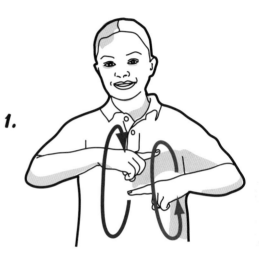

Both hands make the "1" hand shape
and rotate around each other.

Formar el "1" con ambas manos y girar
alrededor de cada una.

Hop
Saltar/Brincar

1.

2.

3.

Fingers spell H-O-P.
Los dedos deletrean H-O-P.

Clap
Aplaudir

1.

Clap hands.
Manos aplauden.

Slide
Resbalar/Deslizar

1.

2.

Right hand (palm facing toward the floor) moves downward in the shape of a slide.

Mover la mano derecha (palma mirando hacia el piso) hacia abajo en forma de resbaladilla.

Break
Romper

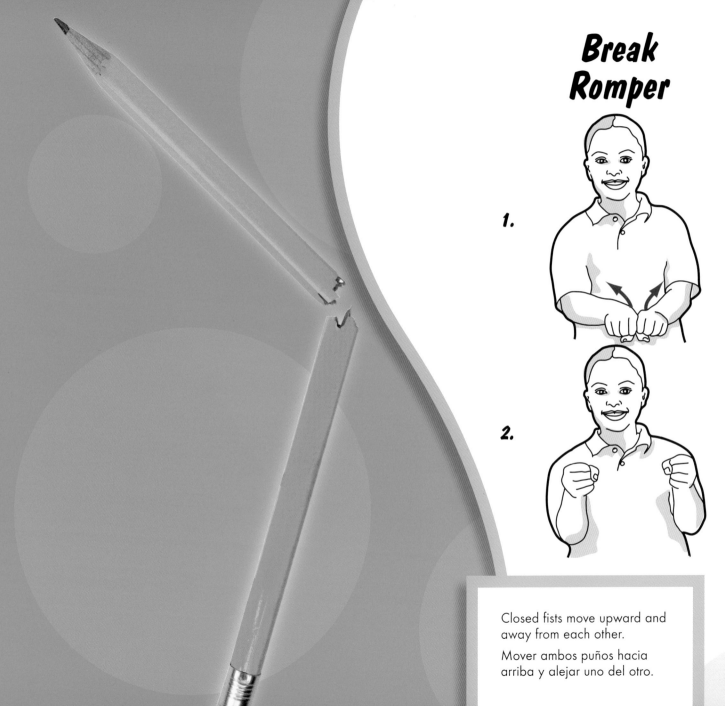

1.

2.

Closed fists move upward and away from each other.

Mover ambos puños hacia arriba y alejar uno del otro.

19

Dig
Excavar

1.

2.

Both hands have closed fists and move in the same direction down and up, as if using a shovel.

Mover ambos puños en la misma dirección hacia abajo y arriba como si estuviera usando una pala.

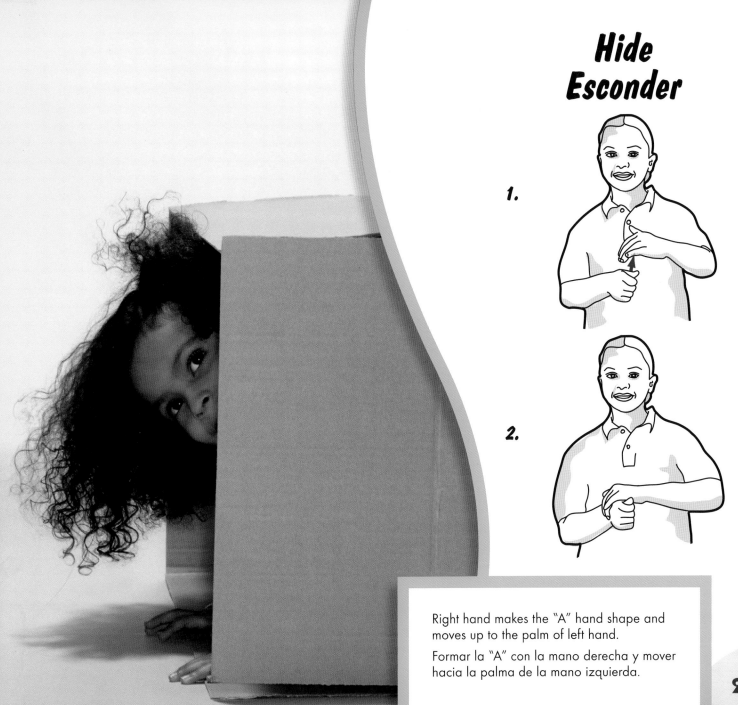

Hide
Esconder

1.

2.

Right hand makes the "A" hand shape and moves up to the palm of left hand.

Formar la "A" con la mano derecha y mover hacia la palma de la mano izquierda.

Cover
Cubrir/Tapar

1.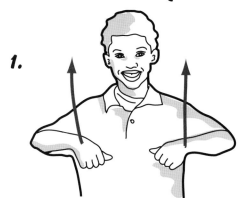

2.

Hands each make the "A" hand shape and move above head, as if covering face with a sheet or blanket.

Formar la "A" con ambas manos y mover arriba de la cabeza como se estuviera cubriendo la cara con una sabana o covertor.

Turn
Vuelta

1.

Right and left hands each make the "1" hand shape. Index fingers of both hands rotate around each other.

Formar el "1" con ambas manos. Los dedos índices de ambas manos rotan.

A B C D E F
G H I J K
L M N O P
Q R S T U
V W X Y Z

Alina is seven years old and is in the second grade. Her favorite things to do are art, soccer, and swimming. DJ is her brother!

Dareous has seven brothers and sisters. He likes football. His favorite team is the Detroit Lions. He also likes to play with his Gameboy and Playstation.

DJ is eight years old and is in the third grade. He loves playing the harmonica and his Gameboy. Alina is his sister!

24